soon out of context

Nigel Baldacchino

Published by Unsolicited Press
www.unsolicitedpress.com

For information, contact publisher at info@unsolicitedpress.com

Unsolicited Press Books are distributed to the trade by Ingram.
Printed in the United States of America.
ISBN: 978-1-947021-84-6

PREFACE

It is of course a truism to say that today we live in an age of distraction: the ceaseless likes, clicks and swipes that impinge on our digital consciousness, the multitudinous, myriad, manifold memes, GIF, tweets that bombard our existence. Instead of our nights lit by the starry constellations, our nocturnal existences are illumined by the glows of our smart phones.

Nigel Baldacchino's *Soon Out of Context* is a child of this age, but it is a rebellious one. It is a child of our age because its sources were culled from the internet, in a site fittingly entitled archive.org, and also because of its miscellaneous nature. But it is also rebellious because as he combs through the archives of our age, he seeks to return us to a more nostalgic, simpler time (of course all nostalgias are imaginary and possibly fictive): he summons the lambent, golden haze world of the once dusty books that you could only find in community libraries, bric-a-brac antique stores, yellowed periodicals that you find in your great aunt's attic. The images that the reader will encounter in the following pages are whimsical, haunting, lyrical, slightly (if that is the right adverb) surrealist, even Dadaist. But the presiding angel of these pages is a calm, beneficent one, rather than a terrifying one of, say, Rilke in the Duino Elegies, or perhaps more fittingly, Benjamin's and Klee's mischievous and apocalyptic Angelus Novus.

What is the relationship between the text on the verso and images on the recto?

For me, white space is a visual fermata, a breath, a moment for meaning to sink in or for the imagination to generate it.

"What is decisive in collecting is that the object is detached from all its original functions in order to enter into the closest conceivable relation to things of the same kind. . . Collecting is a primal phenomenon of study: the student collects knowledge," Walter Benjamin, writes in the Arcades Project. There is a danger that in collecting scrapes of images randomly that this "hoarding" becomes obsessive and messy. But

Nigel manages to remain serene, elegant, and elevated in this oneiropoietic experiment. He is the student of memory that collects dreams.

— **Dr Andrew Hui**, Associate Professor of Literature at Yale-NUS College.

soon out of context

Nigel Baldacchino

I.

a blind-folded witness

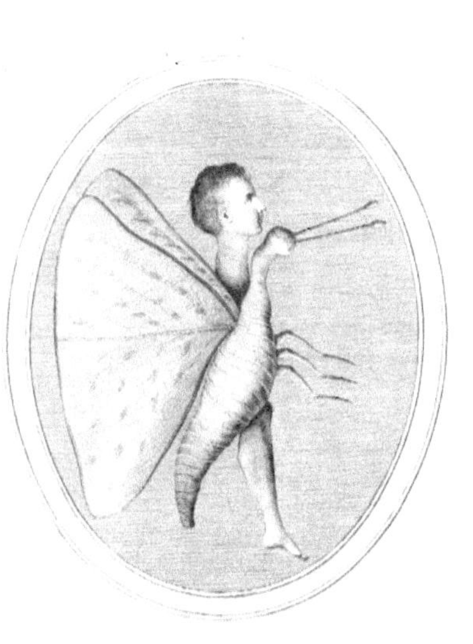

2.

grief is in the eye of the beholder

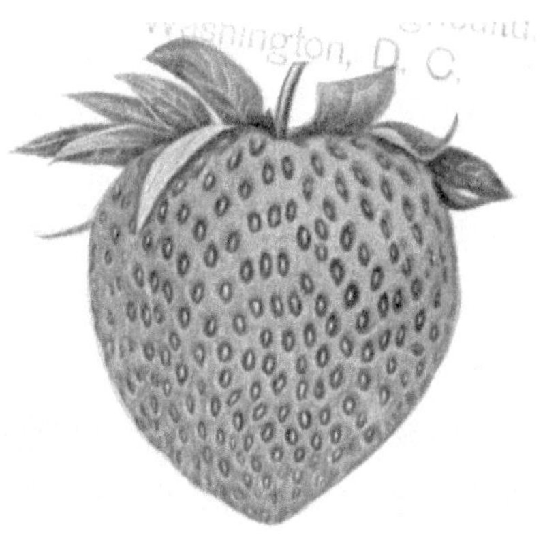

3.

there is no truth when I'm lying by
your side

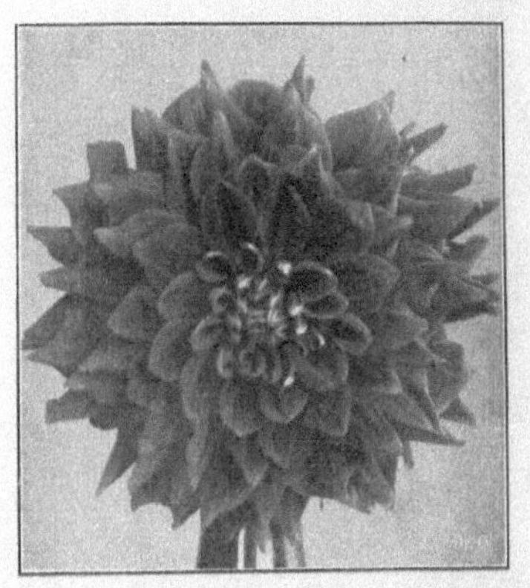

Dahlia H. G. Newman
(New)

Each, $1.00

4.

I teach the sky
to listen to the raindrops
as they die
to the sound of
my prayers

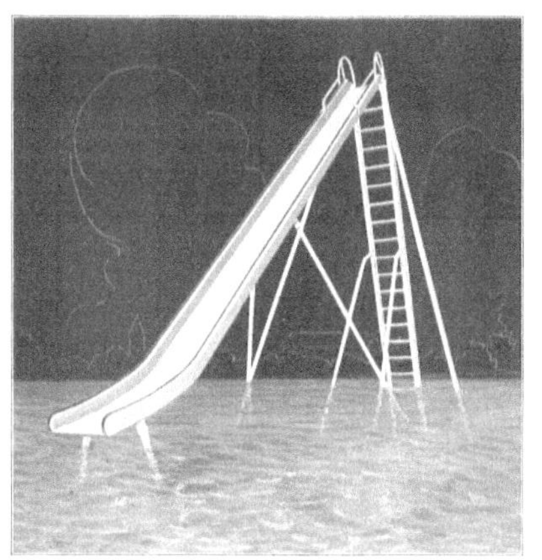

5.

hoping not
to make ends meet

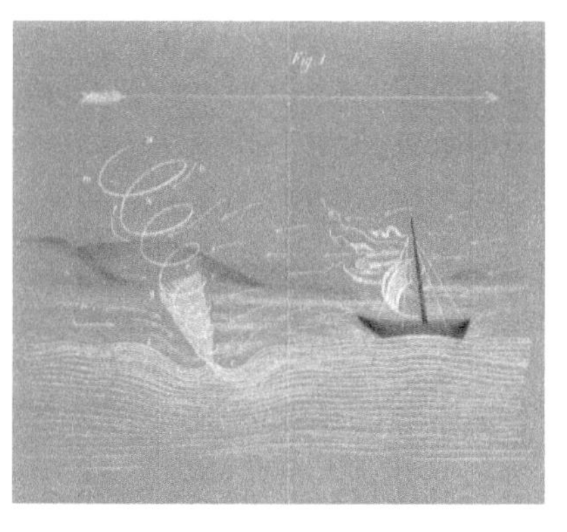
Fig. 1

6.

this clear path killing my fog

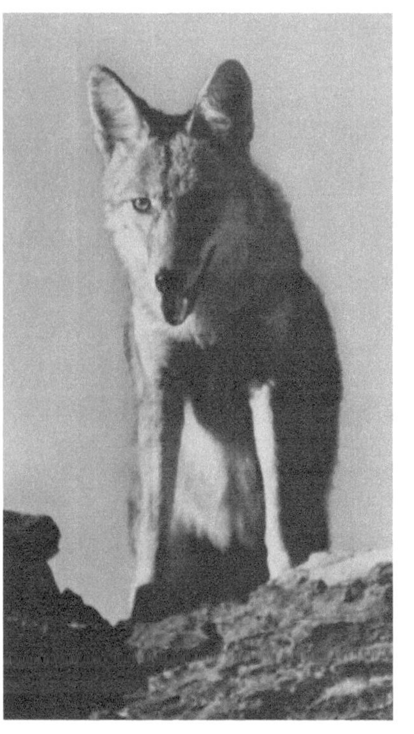

7.

have things ever been how they
used to be?

8.

parallel lines are bound never to
meet
because of something they share

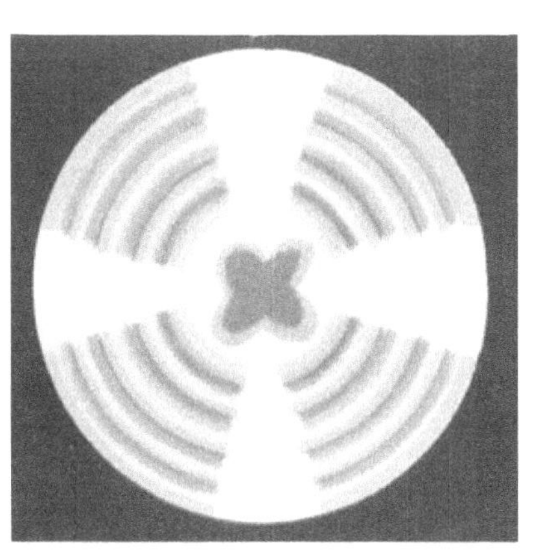

9.

nightmares always turn the other
cheek

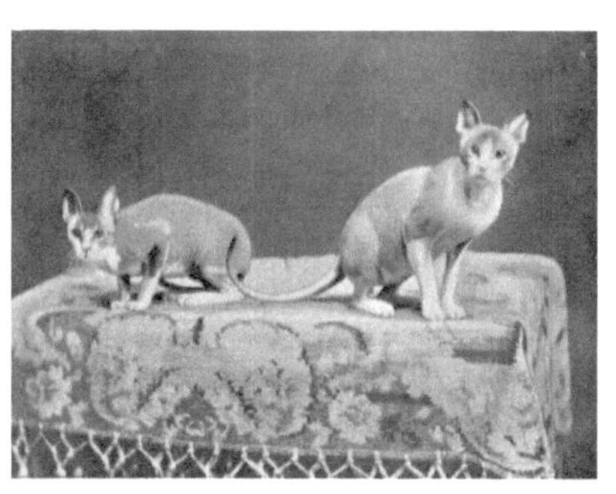

10.

what is exile and why are we alone
here?

Judy is Lost

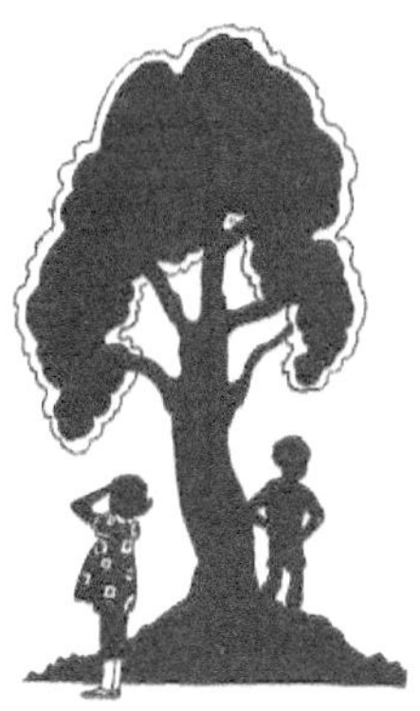

11.

scratching the surface
of a glowing furnace
we sin in peace

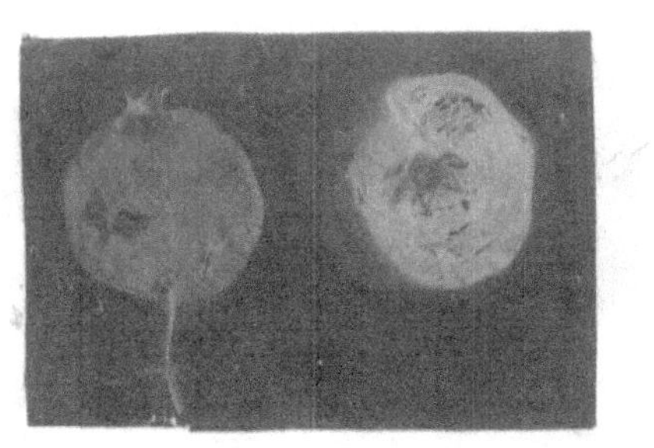

12.

that place in our heart
our nightmares fear

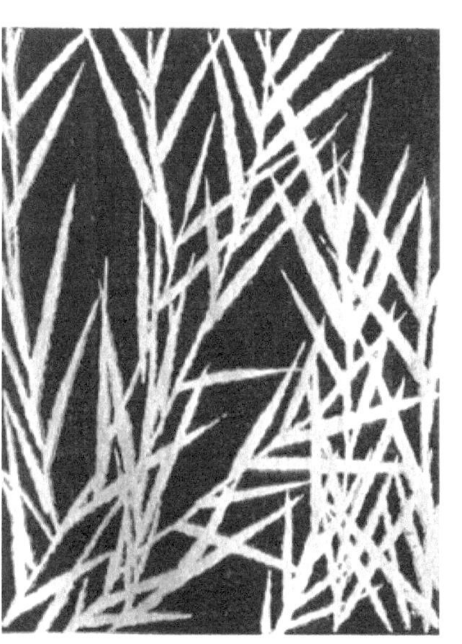

13.

the place in our heart
our loneliness fears

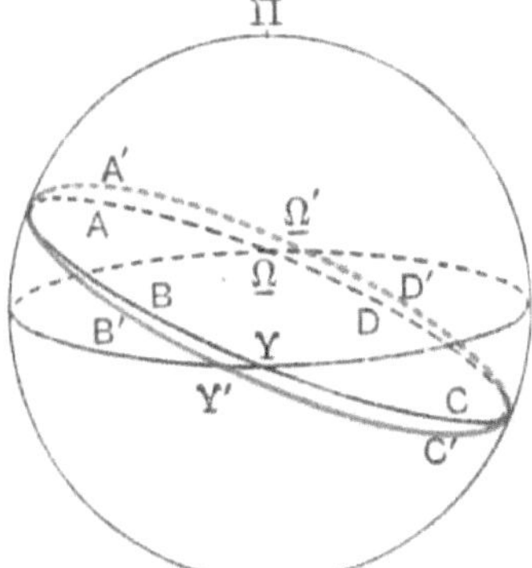

Fig. 23.—The precession of the equinoxes.

14.

you are my first shadow with which
daylight
interferes

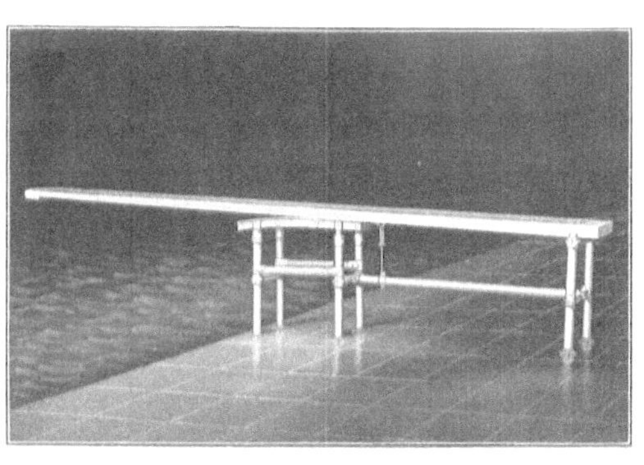

15.

listening to the wind
holding out the candles
long before
they ran out

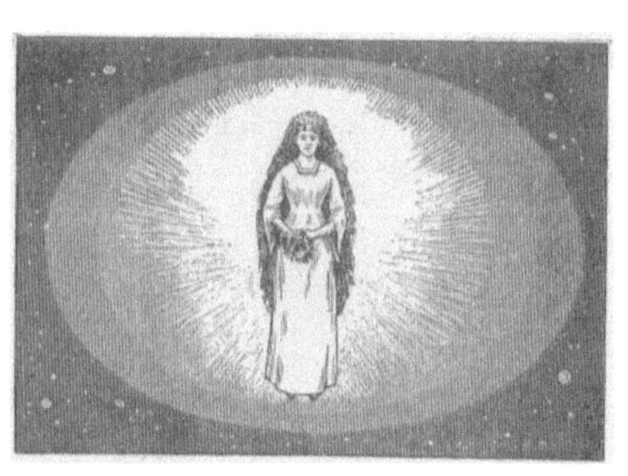

16.

everything lies
in circles

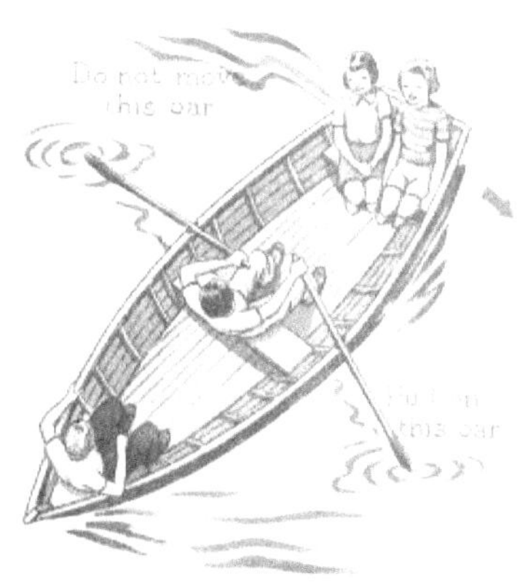
Do not move
this oar
Pull in
this oar

17.

I could feel
your human limits fading
you apologise
you always do

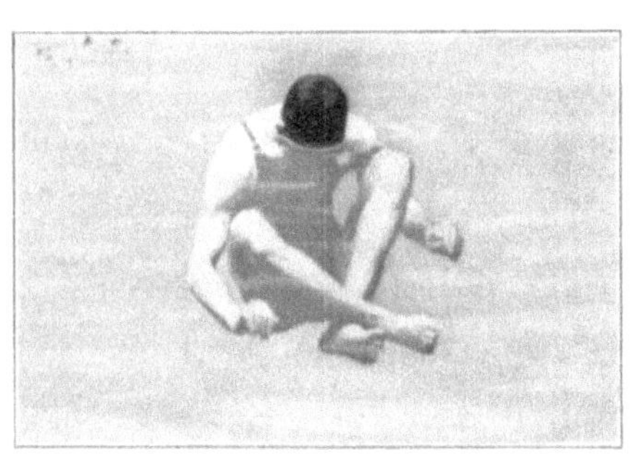

18.

when someone is joyful enough
they cry

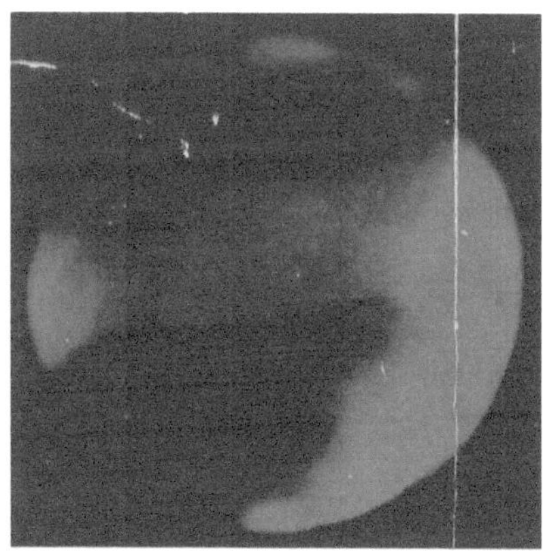

19.

an anchor for a sinking ship

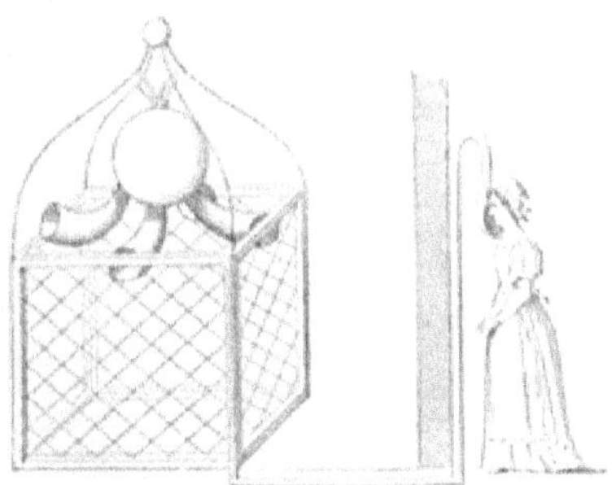

20.

pitch darkness
intense glare
both as blinding

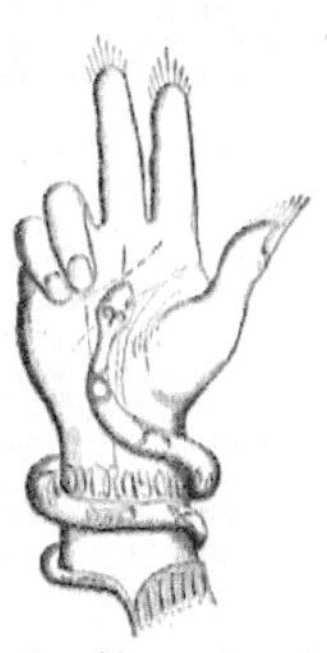

To all in Search of Truth.
Greeting.

21.

think hard and shiver
I expect some truth
in your gentle eyes

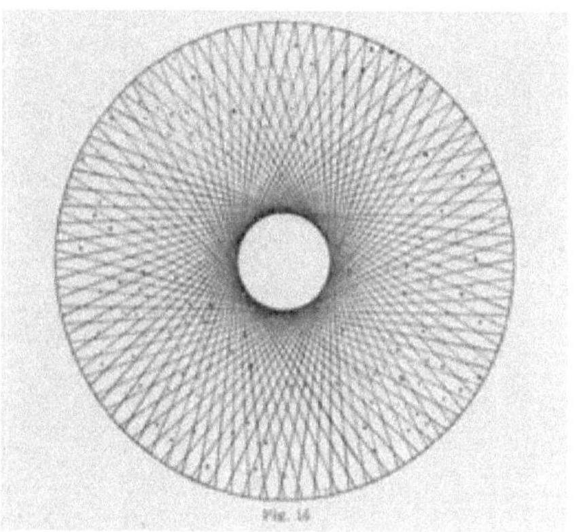

Fig. 16

22.

letting go
I shared with you
the laws of futility

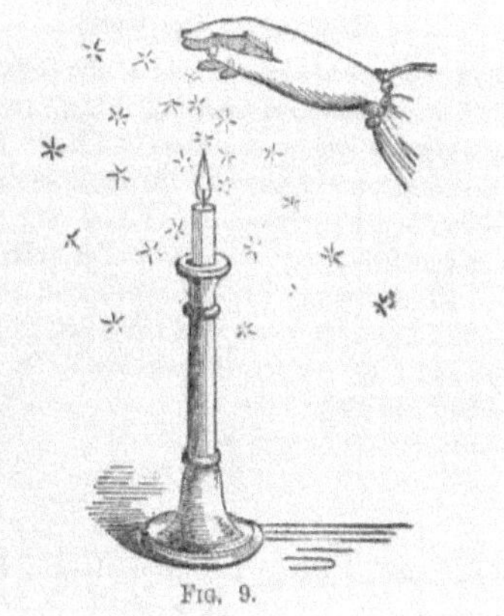

Fig. 9.

23.

stranded in rough seas, rocky
shores are at once one's only hope
and starkest danger

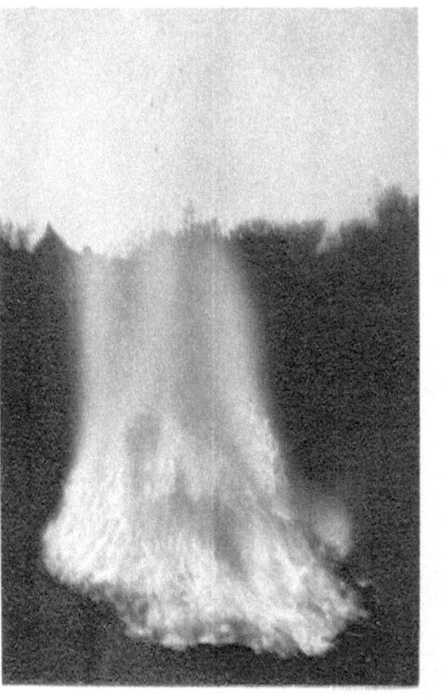

24.

if all goes well
I will suffer

25.

water is composed of Hydrogen
and Oxygen; two of the most
unstable, reactive and volatile
elements

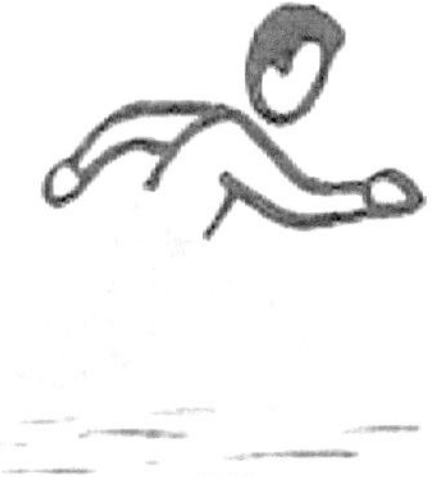

26.

when a sound is constant enough
it is silence

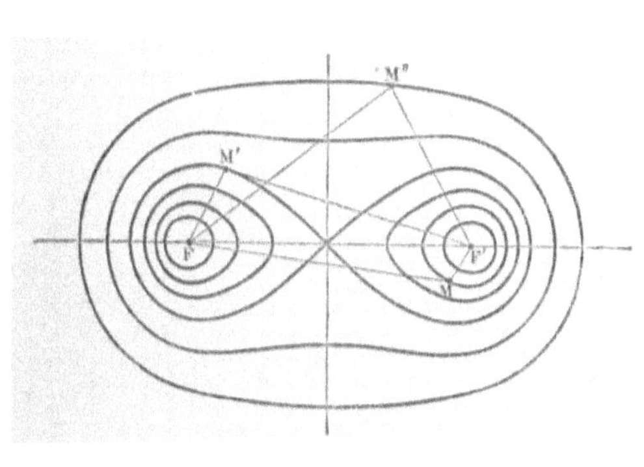

"M"
M'
F'
F'
M

27.

you never listen when I ask if I'm
allowed to pause
to catch my breath

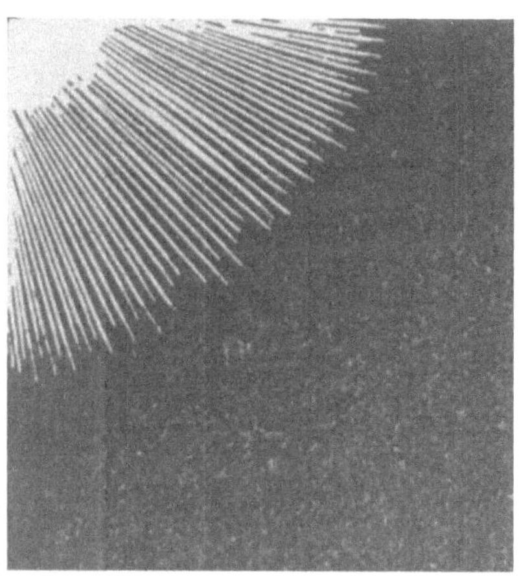

28.

never forgive me
because I never would

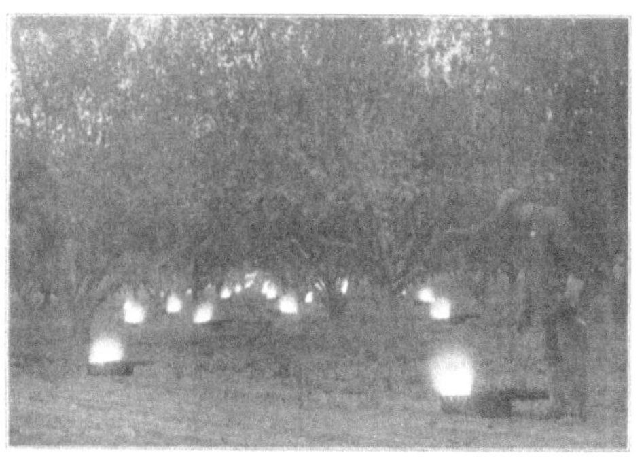

29.

seeps through
our perforated whole,
some air

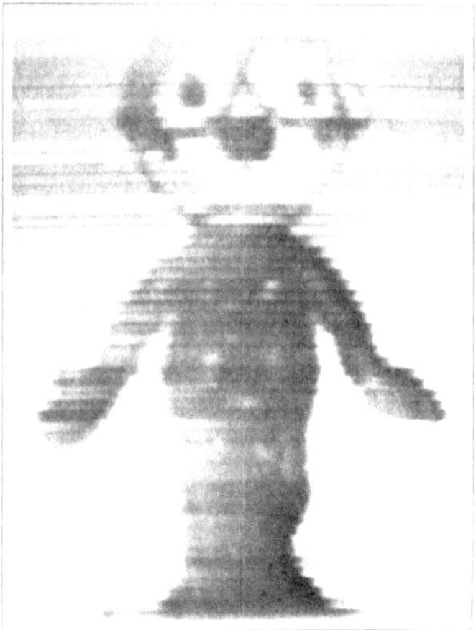

30.

nobody calls
and I never answer

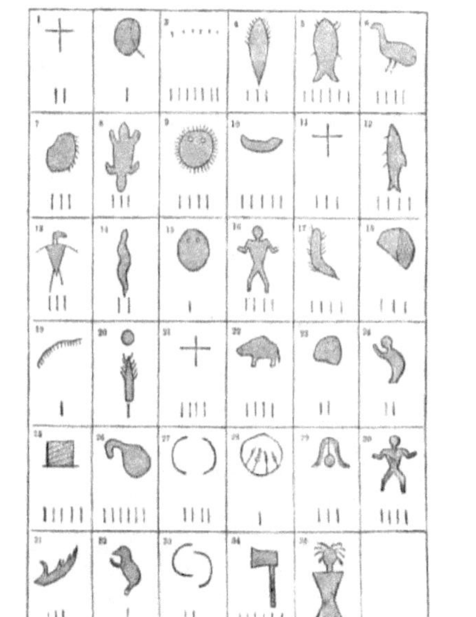

31.

I'm alive
I'm afraid

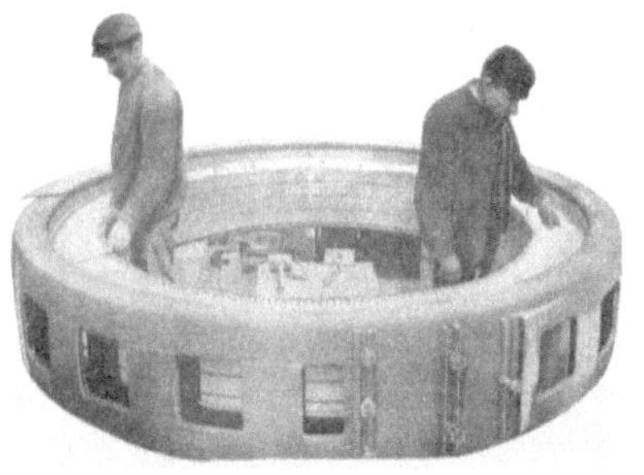

REFERENCES

1.

Alcuni monumenti del Museo Carrafa
Author: Carafa, Giovanni, duca di Noja
Published: ca. 1778 [In Napoli : [s.n.]]

2.

Great crops of strawberries and how to grow them
Author: R.M. Kellogg Co; Henry G. Gilbert Nursery and Seed Trade Catalog Collection
Published: ca. 1928 [Three Rivers, Mich.]

3.

Catalog of dahlias : cactus, show fancy, decorative, peony, flowered, collarette, single and pompom dahlias
Author: Geo. H. Walker; Henry G. Gilbert Nursery and Seed Trade Catalog Collection
Published: ca. 1919 [see author]

4.

Park, Pool and Playground Equipment
Author: American Playground Device Co.
Published: ca. 1935 [see author]

5.

David Rumsey Historical Map Collection

Author: Beron, Pierre
Published: 1860 [Mallet-Bachelier,
Lemercier]

6.
COYOTE. [COURTESY, U. S. FISH AND WILDLIFE SERVICE.] ; The dinosaur quarry : Dinosaur National Monument, Colorado-Utah
Author: John M. Good, Theodore E. White, and Gilbert F. Stucker.
Published: 1958 [Washington, D.C. : National Park Service]

7.
Unkashu
Author: Kōrin Furuya
Published: 1903 [Kyōto-shi : Yamada Unsōdō]

8.
Polarisation of light
Author: Spottiswoode, William, 1825-1883
Published: 1884 [London, Macmillan and co.]

9.
The book of the cat
Author: Miss Frances Simpson

Published: 1903 [Melbourne, Cassell and
company, limited]

10.
**Far Horizons Readers: Play Out of Doors
– Primer**
Author: D. J. Dickie
Published: 1936 [Toronto, J. M. Dent]

11.
Punica granatum L.
Author: Hyden van der Froeschl
Published: via plantillustrations.org

12.
Shin bijutsukai
Author: Kōrin Furuya
Published: 1902 [Meiji 35-nen 5-gatsu
25-nichi]

13.
**The world: or, first lessons in astronomy
and geology, in
connetion with the present and past
condition of our globe**
Author: Hamilton Lanphere Smith
Published: 1848 [M. C. Younglove and co.
]

14.
see 4

15.

Voice from the Heavens, Or Stellar & Celestial Worlds

Author: Reuben Potter
Published: 1890 [Carrier Dove Printingrand Pub. Co]

16.

Exploring Science: Five - Teachers' Edition b

Author: Walter A Thurber
Published: 1957 [Toronto : Macmillan of Canada]

17.

Swimming scientifically taught; a practical manual for young and old Author: Frank

Eugen Dalton
Published: 1912 [New York and London, Funk & Wagnalls company]

18.

Guide to Mars [2nd ed]

Author: Patrick Moore
Published: 1965 [Frederick Muller Ltd.]

19.

The applications of physical forces [microform]

Authors: Amédée Guillemin, Sir Joseph Norman Lockyer

Published: 1877 [Macmillan]

20.
The mystic self : uncommon sense versus common sense
Authors: Mesha Rayon, Harry Houdini Collection
Published: 1900 [Chicago, Ill., U. S. A]

21.
see 13

22.
Book of riddles and five hundred home amusements : containing a choice and curious collection of riddles, charades, enigmas, rebuses, anagrams, transpositions, conundrums, amusing puzzles, queer sleights, recreations in arithmetic, fireside games, and natural magic, embracing entertaining amusements in magnetism, chemistry, second sight, and simple recreations in science for family and social pastime Authors: Wiljalba Frikell, Harry Houdini Collection
Published: 1863 [New York : Dick & Fitzgerald]

23.
Luther Burbank : his methods and discoveries and their practical application

Author: Luther Burbank
Published: Luther Burbank Press [1914-15
]

24.
see 7

25.
Biology in Daily Life
Author: Francis D. Curtis, John Urban
Published: 1953 [Boston, Ginn]

26.
see 8

27.
see 15

28.
**Agricultural meteorology; the effect of
weather on crops**
Author: John Warren Smith
Published: 1920 [Macmillan]

29.
An introduction to television
Authors: Clarence John Hylander, Robert
Harding
Published: 1941 [Macmillan]

30.
The story of the alphabet
Author: Edward Clodd
Published: 1900 [G. Newnes]

31.
Armature construction
Author: Henry Metcalf Hobart
Published: 1907 [Whittaker]

32.
Home fun
Author: Cecil Henry Bullivant
Published: 1910 [Dodge publishing]

ABOUT THE PROJECT

this project involves the work of Nigel Baldacchino in writing, collecting archived images online, and together with his friend Josmar Azzopardi assigning instances of text and summoned images to one another in an attempt to shape a subjective level of extended discourse. Azzopardi also takes the role of an early editor of the written work.

special thanks goes to *nemfrog* [https://nemfrog.tumblr.com/], whose work in sifting through online archives was used on many levels; from helping to inspire the idea for the book, to providing crucial sources for images.

Nigel Baldacchino (b. 1989) is an architect by profession, who also actively produces music, writes poetry, designs books and works with photography. As an architect, Baldacchino notably occupied main roles in design teams for two major museum projects, namely MUŻA (The Malta National Community Art Museum) and St. John's Co-Cathedral Museum. Other architectural works include the setup for NISĠA: Storja Kontemporanja (2018, Valletta), a collective exhibition curated to portray a series of narratives tying modernist and contemporary Maltese art.

In 2012, Baldacchino represented Malta in BOZAR EXPO: Sense of Place, an international collective photography exhibition curated by Liz Wells, alongside photographers such as Massimo Vitali and Andreas Gursky. The exhibition was documented in an extensive published catalogue bearing the same name. Other photography exhibitions include *In Transit* (2017, Düsseldorf/Leeuwarden) and *VIVA: Inside the Fragment* (2017, Valletta). In 2018 he joined the Oliver Gordon Gallery as a resident photographer and had a selection of work included in the National Collection (MUŻA). Baldacchino's photography was also compiled in a publication by EDE books as part of their Photo Book series.

In parallel, Baldacchino started working on music in 2011 through his musical project *Fastidju*, developing rough musical and written ideas with local producers. The project eventually developed into a band that performed several times around the island and released a self titled album in 2014. Solo self-produced work soon followed suit, culminating in a number of soundtracks for theatre and video art. Videos include Adrian Abela's *4.1868 The Theory of Heat (2013)* and *SONUS: The sound of sonnets and the paper memory machine (2015)*; whereas theatre performances include Teatru Santwarju's *LIMBUS* (2018) and Rebecca Camilleri/Nicola Rayworth's *S-S-Spaces (2013)*.

The written ideas devised as lyrical content for the band, meanwhile, slowly started developing their own artistic character, eventually piling up and branching out into creative writing projects.

Andrew Hui teaches literature and the humanities at Yale-NUS College, Singapore. He loves to read and talk to people about art, culture and ideas, and is the author of *The Poetics of Ruins in Renaissance Literature* and *A Theory of the Aphorism from Confucius to Twitter*.